Revelation Unpacked

Les Marsh

D1434213

Copyright © 2015 Les Marsh

Published in 2015 by Wide Margin,

90 Sandyleaze, Gloucester, GL2 0PX, UK

`http://www.wide-margin.co.uk/`

ISBN 978-1-908860-14-9

Printed and bound in Great Britain by
Lightning Source, Milton Keynes

Revelation Unpacked

Table of Contents

Translator's thanks

I am totally indebted to the many scholars who have served me so graciously throughout my life. These include, from my boyhood, the privilege of having as my father, H G Marsh. Then from undergraduate days, Kenneth Grayston (with the old NEB), and all through to today Tom Wright (with *The New Testament for Everyone*). They would doubtless express their indebtedness to all those working in the field. The value in this work, of course, is theirs; any errors are mine.

This translation has come out of the seminars for Oxford postgraduates which I have been facilitating for the past four years. I must thank them for their constant encouragement, and for their help in honing the text into a meaningful shape.

Its publication has only been made possible through the editing of Heidi Cottrell, and my unbounded gratitude is due to her and to her gracious husband Andrew. Equally immense thanks are due to Heather Lang for another of her perfect cover designs.

Translator's thanks

Before we begin...

Even enthusiastic Christians are apt to shy away from the book of Revelation. Privately, they may even think it slightly mad, certainly well over the top, and obscure into the bargain. Many of us would echo Martin Luther's reaction:

> The book of Revelation tells us to 'keep what it says'. But no one knows what it says!

At least, we can all agree that if it's prophecy, it's not like any prophecy we know. The prophets in the Bible spoke plainly:

> The Lord says you shall not cheat... steal... kill...

But these early plain-speaking prophets tended to end up dead.

Later prophets wrote in a way that their overlords wouldn't understand. What they wrote would make as little sense to their rulers as it does to us. Only those they wrote it for would grasp the meaning. John, the author of the book of Revelation, writes in this 'apocalyptic' style.

John's 'apocalypse' uses symbols and code, which we have to unpack. This translation aims to unpack it for us, and to uncover 'what John is saying' in plain English. It unpacks the symbols, it decodes, it fills in the context, and exposes what is implied. John's Revelation is then itself revealed. His breath-taking story becomes an open book. The great finale of the Bible is unlocked for everyone to read.

Alice in Wonderland...

Yet even in an unpacked translation we may at times feel a bit like Alice in Wonderland. Things can appear to be upside down. We discover that the Messiah-Jesus' followers—tiny groups of persecuted and powerless people—are seen by John as the rulers! How could anyone imagine anything so absurd?

But John is claiming to look from God's point of view, and the absurdity comes directly from Jesus. Several of Jesus' first motley gang of followers had themselves wanted to be the rulers. On the very night Jesus was betrayed and arrested, they quarrelled over who was next in line. So he told them:

> You call me the ruler and the leader, and you're right, for that's what I am. But I act like your slave.
>
> Godless rulers exploit and boss people about; that's not how it's to be with you. I've given you an example, [washing your feet]. Among you the ruler must be like the least important; the leader who behaves as if he were a servant. My Father gave me my authority to rule. I give you authority to rule in the same way.

So John sees Jesus' followers, the least well-regarded in society, as the rulers in God's eyes—but rulers in Jesus' way like servants, loving and acting as he did.

What is 'God's point of view'?

John found 'God's point of view' in the life and mind of Jesus. For Jesus had done God's job: the job of cleaning up the mess made of God's creation by humans. The big story—of the Creator and his creation—is told in the Bible. The book of Revelation is the last chapter of the story, which began in Genesis when...

The big story

...the good Creator decided to make a garden-city-paradise on earth, to live with his people. But, led astray by evil, his people thought they'd build the city for themselves. As a result, they ended up in the chaos of Babel and the slavery of Babylon.

To cure the problem God made a covenant with Abraham and his family, the Jews. They would follow God's plan to make life heaven-on-earth for every family. But they broke the covenant, bowed down to idols, and ended up completely lost.

Of course, God didn't break his covenant; he kept it by sending the promised Jewish Messiah (King). That Messiah, Jesus, set up God's rule on earth for ever.

But the way Jesus did it upturned everyone's ideas of both God and his rule. If his 'rule' was now in place, it left a lot of questions for the Messiah's followers.

Why did bad things still happen?

The Roman emperor still held sway, and the Messiah's followers were outcasts. At any moment they could be attacked by vicious mobs, or arrested, imprisoned and executed. If you didn't worship the divine Roman emperor, you were not allowed to trade—and if you couldn't trade, you starved. The followers of the Messiah wondered where they had got to in the Bible's story.

John's book is a glorious bracing answer to all their questions. It tells them how to act in the new situation, and foretells the future. It offers them a hope-giving answer for the future of all humanity.

Scholars think it was written by 95 AD, though we can't be sure. We are sure what the neighbouring Roman governor, named Pliny, wrote to the emperor 15 years later. His letter claimed that all the temples of the emperor's gods were deserted, due to 'Christians'. So he set about wiping these 'Christians' out.

These 'Christians' would have been like the ones John is writing for, ordinary people with ordinary struggles. They were different because something extraordinary had happened to them. This brought them persecution by the establishment because they had 'turned the world upside down'!

They had in fact turned emperor-worship, male domination, slavery, violence, and all racial privilege on its head. They had replaced these imperial 'virtues' with 'evil things' like equal standing, a good conscience, freedom, and true humanity. The establishment's response:

'Away with such people from the earth!'

His forecast

But does John's answer and forecast of the future stand up? After all, we know that forecasters today—political, financial or other—can't even forecast a few months ahead. So it comes as a surprise to find someone who 'got it right' for two millennia, right up to today.

Yet it seems as if no book in history has been more misunderstood. An internet search for 'Revelation' offers tens of millions of results: it's everything from 'war literature' to 'an erotic mystery of power and sex'! Many think it predicts 'the end of the world'. It may be a relief to know that it does no such thing.

It's because it is not about the end of the world, that Revelation is so relevant today. John's forecast was rooted in our humanity, with our good and bad choices. So his great finale is not an escape from this world, or a man-made utopia—he was a very earthy realist —but a Jesus-centred dream for people like us.

That dream, of a world of unselfish people as a free gift from God, comes from John's trust in a good Creator, whose nature is self-denying love. That burning conviction was all based on the hard evidence of Jesus' self-sacrificial victory on the cross. His resurrection made certain that his rule would prevail.

It's all happening at once!

In John's Revelation, the excitement mounts. First come the seals, then the trumpets, and after the trumpets, the plagues. But John is not pretending that they happen in a very neat order. That's not the way things are in the real world. What he writes is to be understood as all happening at the same time.

Such things were happening as he wrote, and they have continued, as he prophesied, to the present. Yet along with them there are the signs of the final ending of the story. The one thing to which we look forward is the final transformation: from the earth as we see it today, to the new earth and heavens as they will be in the future.

Who was this John?

About thirty years after Revelation was written, there was a memorial to John in Ephesus, one of the great cities of the ancient world. It had a quarter of a million people, and John writes a letter to the Christians there. But at that time it held memorials to two Johns! So who were they?

Tradition tells us that the John of Revelation was one of Jesus' right-hand men. But 200 years later someone said, 'this is not like John's Gospel so it can't be by him'. Today, many scholars agree that John's Gospel was written by a different John. So which John wrote which book we can't be sure.

Whoever wrote it, what matters for us is whether what it says is relevant and rings true. This, each of us must discover for ourselves. But one thing we can say with confidence. In a world saturated with depressing news, it offers fresh hope for anyone who asks the questions:

• *What's really happening here on earth?*

• *Why is it happening?*

• *What will be the outcome?*

• *What are we to do about it?*

Synopsis

John was exiled on a rocky Greek island off the coast of Turkey. There he had a vision of Jesus, the earth's ruler, caring for all his persecuted churches. John was told by Jesus to write to encourage all the churches. He was then invited into 'the earth's operations centre' to be shown what was happening on earth. There, he saw beyond outward appearances, to what was really going on in the world. This he was told to pass on to all God's servants.

Then, in the light of the self-sacrificial victory of Jesus, John glimpsed the future. People would continue to build empires, make wars, and cause economic crashes, pain and death. Their behaviour would bring about the breakdown and destruction of societies. But through it all, God's people would share the Messiah's victory over evil.

God's response to inhuman behaviour would be seen by its consequences—damage to the environment, and humanity's worst nightmares. These should warn people to alter their behaviour, but people would refuse to change their ways.

The prophetic role of John and the churches would be to overcome evil through suffering. In this way they would proclaim that Jesus was the earth's supreme ruler. Their faithful witness to him would save the lives of countless millions.

It was then revealed to John that human problems were not haphazard. They were part of evil's plan to destroy God's good creation. Evil was determined to destroy the church because the Messiah's church upset evil's plan. Imperial domination and its acolytes were the tools evil used. But evil had been critically wounded by Jesus' victory over it on the cross. His self-sacrifice in love, and that of his followers, fed a life-giving stream to heal the nations.

God had used the plagues of Egypt to free his people from slavery. So even plagues can be God's harbingers of freedom for his people. For evil brings its own destruction; it is 'the destroyer': it destroys its own.

11

Evil empires are built on shaky foundations, and are bound to collapse. In reality, the Messiah's people now reign on earth throughout the present age. Overcoming evil through suffering, their share in the victory is assured. Only at the final judgement will every trace of evil be removed.

With sure hope we await God's fullest gifts, in a new society impregnable to fear. Then, wonderful beyond words, God will be wholly present in it, and all earth's wrongs healed. With heaven come on earth, all nations will be drawn to it, and everyone welcomed into it. God's plan from the beginning—to dwell with his people for ever in a garden-city-paradise on earth—will be realised.

But the Messiah's people are not only promised this future. They are, says John, offered a foretaste of this gift now. It is already in process, and everyone has the choice and chance to share in it.

Revelation Unpacked:
An Easy To Read Translation

The Introduction

Revealed!

1 ¹ The earth's ruler, Jesus, has revealed what's really happening, and what's going to happen... and why. Through Jesus, God has opened up what is to come for his servants. He has shown it to his servant John, who wrote it in this book. ² John vouches for it as God's word. Everything he saw is the evidence of the supreme ruler Jesus, coming from God. ³ Those who read it, grasp what it says and act on it, enter the new world. What it foretells is already in process. ⁴ This letter comes from John to every church, via the churches of southeast Turkey.

I know how you are suffering

My prayer for you, especially under persecution, is this:

> *May God's free gift of winning, pure, generous love of others, and peace of heart be yours. He was and is always present, and always will be.*
>
> *May his Holy Spirit provide every gift you need.*
>
> ⁵ *May Jesus, faithful in the face of death, and first to rise from death, be with you. He is ruler of all rulers on earth. He loves us, and gave his life to liberate us from evil.* ⁶ *He has made us rulers with him, to turn the nations to God his Father. Glory and power are his for ever. That's for sure.*

⁷ Feast your eyes on the winner! As the prophet said, everyone will recognise their ruler, even 'those who killed him'. Every tribe on earth is going to be truly sorry, for how they've treated him. That is certain.

⁸ God declares:
I, the eternal all-powerful, am the beginning and goal of everything.

The vision

⁹ I, John, your brother, share your hardships, your status as rulers, and your perseverance through suffering as Jesus' people. The Bible promised suffering for the Messiah and his followers, as Jesus bore witness. I was suffering exile on Patmos Island, ¹⁰ and one Sunday I was swept away by the Spirit. I heard a great voice behind me, like a trumpet call:

¹¹ 'Write down in a book,' the voice said, 'what you see. Send it to the whole church, through the seven churches in southwest Turkey.'

¹² I turned to see who was speaking to me, and saw a vision. It was of the churches, ¹³ with Jesus at the centre of them, victorious, giving them courage. ¹⁴ He shone with God's wisdom, and his eyes blazed with justice. ¹⁵ His beauty dazzled right down to his feet, and his voice spoke with irresistible power. ¹⁶ His right hand held messages for his churches, with words cutting sharper than the sharpest sword. His appearance was as bright as the sun.

¹⁷ 'No man can look on God and live,' says *The Law*.

So when I saw him, I dropped like a dead man. But he put his hand on me, and took my fear away.

'Have no fear!' he said. 'I am the Creator, and I have the last word. ¹⁸ I died, and look! I am alive to endless ages. I hold the key to death and the world of the dead. ¹⁹ So write what you see, both what is happening, and what is going to happen. ²⁰ I have messages for you to send to all the churches.

To the 'successful'

2 ¹ 'Write to the church in Ephesus:

² This comes from the One who is always with you.

I know all you've done. I know the problems you've faced, and the resilience you've shown. You don't put up with frauds, and you see through scroungers, who come claiming to be 'apostles'. ³ You face persecution with true human dignity. You suffer much for following me, and you don't give in.

⁴ My deep concern is that you've given up the love you started with. ⁵ Look back, and see how far you've fallen. Rethink what you're doing, and practice love in your actions, as you did in the beginning. If you don't, there won't be an Ephesian church much longer. ⁶ But I'll say this for you. You don't confuse love with sex-worship, and nor do I.

⁷ Your city's temple is one of the seven wonders of the world. Its beautiful garden has a 'tree of life". Any condemned criminal who reaches it, saves his life. But I give anyone facing death for my sake fruit from the tree of real life. That tree is with God, in the paradise of God's garden.

Let those who will listen, hear what the Spirit is saying to the churches.

For the poorest—who are richest!

[8]'Write to the church in Smyrna, a city resurrected after the earthquake:

> This comes from the first to be resurrected, whose resurrection ensures the final resurrection.
>
> [9] I feel your suffering, and your poverty in a wealthy city —though you're the really rich! I know the lies people, who claim to be Jews, tell about you. They're not real Jews; they're doing the work of the great deceiver, Satan. [10] So don't be afraid of what you have to suffer. Evil plots will have some of you thrown in prison, to break your faith. You may have to suffer torture for some time.
>
> Your town boasts a crown of hill-top buildings, but the crown of life is what I give. Those faithful to me in the face of death, receive it. [11] No one can take away their share in the age to come.
>
> Let those who listen, hear what the Spirit is saying to the churches.

To those in great danger

[12]'Write to the church in Pergamum, seat of the Roman Governor, who boasts of his sharp sword:

> This comes from Jesus, whose sword cuts deepest—even to the thoughts of the heart:

¹³ I know you have kept faithful to me, right under the nose of the Roman Governor. He embodies the evil empire. But you didn't renounce my authority, even when he martyred my faithful witness Antipas in your midst. I know what you have to face.

¹⁴ But you do have faults. Some of you have been trapped into idolatry, by those who teach that "adultery is love". They've lost the plot, and joined those who worship their feelings. ¹⁵ You've got others too with similar corrupt teaching. ¹⁶ So think again, before disaster strikes your church. My words will quickly cut through to what's really at stake in these issues.

¹⁷ Your city is built of local black stone. Tickets for your civic banquets have your name on a white stone. But I give a white ticket of victory, to those who face death and conquer it. It's a ticket to my secret banquet. It is the gift of the most intimate relationship with me, for those persecuted for my sake.

If you can hear this, listen to what the Spirit is saying to the churches.

To the easily confused

¹⁸ 'Write to the church in Thyatira, whose blazing furnaces turn out shining metal:

This comes from the ruler, whose eyes blaze with love; who gives justice and peace.

[19] I know all you've done: your love, faithfulness, service, and true human dignity. I know that you're now working harder than ever. [20] But you make one mistake. You let a fashionable lady, who claims to be "prophetic", teach and deceive my people. She tells them to sleep around, and compromise with pagan idol-worship like everyone else.

[21] She's had plenty of time to think again, but she doesn't want to stop sleeping around. [22] So she'll end up with the painful consequences, and so will her pupils. Unless they think again, [23] they too are on the road to death. All the churches will come to realise that I search hearts and minds. Each one will get what they're living for.

[24] I've nothing else against the rest of you who reject her teaching. You haven't worshipped the god of metal, and engaged in what they call "the deep things of Satan". You don't need any more instructions. [25] Just keep a firm grip on what you have, ready for my final victory.

[26] Those against you boast of their power. But anyone who conquers death my way will rule the earth. [27] My people will have power to overcome suffering and death, as scripture puts it, like "your metal rods have power to smash clay pots". [28] I will give them my royal authority which I received from my Father. I will make them radiant as the dawn of a new day.

[29] If you can hear this, listen to what the Spirit is saying to the churches.

To any who think they can't fall

3 [1] 'Write to the church in Sardis, the city that thought it could never fall:

But it did!

So do you think you can't fall? This comes from One who is all-wise, all-powerful, and all-caring for the churches.

I know the things you've done, and your reputation for being alive—but you're dead! [2] Wake up! Strengthen what's left of you, which is half-dead already. You've brought no one to complete commitment to me. [3] Think back to how you received the great news and acted on it. Keep to it, and sort your thinking out! If you don't watch out, when persecution strikes you'll fall like your city did. And it could happen at any time.

[4] I can name a few of you who haven't soiled themselves. They are fit to share my victory over evil. [5] They have overcome the pressure to worship idols, and will share the fruits of victory with me. They will certainly not be wiped out. On the day of judgement, I will stand up for them before my father.

[6] Let anyone with ears listen, to what the Spirit is saying to the churches.

To those being given opportunities

[7] 'Write to the church in Philadelphia:

These are the words of the one with no ulterior motive, who speaks the truth—the one who holds the key to everything. What he opens, no one can shut. His authority is final.

[8] I know what you do. Look! I'm giving you new openings, and no one will be able to stop you. Though you're not strong, you have kept true to me. You haven't disowned me, even under persecution. [9] Your persecutors are from a synagogue led astray by evil. They claim to be Jews but they're frauds, not real Jews. I'll deal with them. Watch me expose their arrogance, and show them that you are the real people of God.

[10] You have put my message into practice—showing patient hope and truly-human dignity under persecution—so I'll save you from the test that everyone is going to have to face. [11] It'll come soon enough. Keep going the way you are, so no one can challenge the authority with which you speak.

[12] All the pillars of your town's temples collapsed in the earthquake. But those standing fast under persecution, I will make living pillars in the temple of my God. They will stand firm, and never collapse. I will label them 'God's property', in the New Jerusalem, the God-given city. In that new society of heaven on earth, you will have the closest relationship to me

[13] Let anyone with ears listen, to what the Spirit is saying to the churches.

To the wealthy

[14] 'Write to the church in Laodicea—the town that boasts of its bankers and its sheep's pricey black wool—so rich it refused the emperor's help to rebuild after the earthquake!

These are the words of One who has the final word, the catalyst of all creation. He is the One who bore faithful and true witness to God:
[15] I know what you're like. You're like your town's water supply, neither hot nor cold. If only you were hot or cold! [16] Your being tepid makes me sick. [17] Like your town you say, "I'm rich. I've got it all. I don't need anything!"

Your town claims its famed eye-ointment makes people see. You'd better use some! You can't even see yourselves-how spiritually poverty-stricken, morally naked and pitiable you are.

[18] I advise you to buy my real wealth, refined in the fire of persecution. I'll replace your black designer outfits from your famous black sheep with the white robes of a martyr's victory. That will hide the shame of your naked ineffectiveness. Try using my eye ointment of purity, then you'll be able to see. [19] I correct and discipline those I love. Pull yourselves together and get serious!

[20] Look, I'm giving you a choice. Face all the consequences of the way you're going, or welcome me and my way. I'm at your door knocking. If you allow me in, I'll come in and we'll celebrate together. [21] With those faithful under persecution I'll share my seat of power—just as I was faithful, and rule with my Father.

²² Let anyone with ears listen, to what the Spirit says to the churches.'

The First Revelation

What is happening?

What is going to happen?

Inside the earth's operations centre

4 [1] After this, I saw an open door into the earth's operations centre. I heard again the trumpet-like voice that spoke to me earlier.

'Step up here,' the voice said. 'I'll show you what's going to happen.'

[2] At once, the Spirit took me into the earth's operations centre, and I saw the seat of power. [3] The appearance of the One there shone with divine beauty, radiating mercy. [4] Before him were those with true humanity, suffering inhuman persecution on earth. Victorious over their suffering, free of fear and hate, they share his rule.

[5] Awe-inspiring sound and brilliance prefaced his revelation of the future. His Spirit was alight with perfect wisdom, understanding, counsel, strength, knowledge and humility. [6] Before him, evil lay powerless. All his creation was around the throne: [7] the wild and domestic animals and birds, and the people spiritually deprived. [8] Day and night without ceasing, his creatures keep watch and sing:

'Almighty God is the holiest. He has always been, is always, and will be for ever.'

[9] These unthinking creatures simply reflect his glory and honour. That's how they give thanks to the eternal One, who rules for ev-

er. [10] They are joined by his thinking people, who offer their reasoned worship to him. They give their wills to do his will, and proclaim:

[11] 'You deserve glory, honour and power, our God and ruler, because you created everything. Through your will all that is has come about, and came into existence.'

Who knows what the future will bring?

5 [1] The One in the seat of power had a scroll in his right hand. And I saw that the plan for the future was written in it. But it was sealed with seven perfect seals, so that no one could see the future. [2] A call went out everywhere:

'Is anyone able to break these seals, and reveal the future?'

[3] There was no reply. No one anywhere, alive or dead, was able to break the seals. [4] And I was in tears, because no one could tell when our suffering would end. [5] But then one of the faithful told me:

'Dry your tears! Our ruler is the one long-promised. He has the strength of a lion. Look! He has defeated the great deceiver, our enemy, and launched the great future for us. He can break the unbreakable seals, and reveal what is to come.'

[6] I looked to see this lion and saw, standing at the heart of power, a 'slaughtered Lamb'! It was Jesus, the crucified and resurrected One, now the centre of everything. His all-powerful, all-seeing, perfect Spirit of God was now sent out to reach all the earth.

[7] Jesus' victory on the cross secured the future for us. [8] As he did so, the music and prayers of his people rose up, and all his creatures joined his people to acclaim him ruler. [9] Now they sing a new song:

'You are fit to reveal the future; for you gave your life to free people from evil. Your sacrifice drew people of every community, language and nation to God. [10] You made them rulers, to rule the earth God's way and turn all people to you.'

[11] I saw and heard the sound of all his messengers and creatures and people round his throne. They were countless in number, [12] singing their hearts out:

'Jesus, through his self-sacrificial victory, deserves the seat of power. To him belong wealth, wisdom, strength, honour, glory, and praise.'

[13] Then every creature, above, on or under the ground or in the sea, everyone everywhere sang:

'Praise, thanks, honour, glory, and power, belong to God and Jesus, for ever and ever!'

All his creation echoed:

'Yes!!!'

And his people worshipped God.

Jesus reveals the future: injustice brings tragedy

6 [1] Then Jesus broke the first seal, and began to open the future to me. At once, the consequences of people's inhumanity became all too clear. [2] First, men wanting to be 'King of the jungle' appeared, out to conquer and dominate. They were exploiting power to build empire after empire for themselves.

[3] Jesus broke the second seal and there were young bulls lusting for a fight. [4] Ruled by pride, selfish gain, hate and revenge, they were ready to kill and massacre. War followed war, as neighbours and nations fought against each other. Even the pretence of peace on the earth was abandoned.

[5] Then Jesus broke the third seal, and exposed the continual cost of corruption. Dishonest, exploitative dealing, fuelled by greed and fear, went on bringing economic crashes. [6] The price was always to be paid by the poor's intense suffering—while nothing was allowed to harm the lifestyle of the rich.

[7] As Jesus broke the fourth seal, I had a vision of a vulture, circling over the doomed. [8] Pale and sickly death hung over the land, waiting to drag its victims down to its dungeon. Pandemics, famine, murder and disasters would keep on plaguing the earth.

[9] When Jesus broke the fifth seal, I saw those closest to him, his martyrs. [10] Their suffering cried out to God at the injustice done to them:

'Sovereign ruler, you are pure and true. You rule over everything. How long, before you put right all the wrongs on earth? How long will you let people think that "might is right"?'

[11] They were assured that they could relax for a while. They had won the victory, and final justice on earth would come. But many more of their brothers and sisters would yet be martyred and join them.

[12] After Jesus broke the sixth seal, I foresaw the tragic consequences of all the injustice. Nations were shaken to pieces, and societies ripped apart. [13] Across the earth, all that people believed secure was taken away and anarchy took over. [14] People began to think that the end of the world had come.

[15] Rulers, governors, generals, corporate bosses, gangsters, 'the great and the good', like everyone else became desperate. [16] They were looking everywhere to escape, and hide their money. But there was nowhere to hide, and life was unbearable.

[16] 'Bury us!' they pleaded to the mountains and the rocks. 'We'll do anything to avoid facing the truth, and looking into the loving eyes of Jesus.'

[17] But the consequences had caught up with them, and there was no escape.

God keeps his people's hope secure

7 [1] Then I saw that God was protecting the whole earth, both humans and nature, from total devastation.

[2] I saw the dawn of the new day arriving, as God began to mark out his people. By his powerful command, [3] he secures his people in spite of any global disaster.

[4-8] I heard how many people were his. There were the apostles, multiplied by the communities of those who believed through them, multiplied past counting! Each one was known by name. [9] Suddenly, I saw them all—a countless number—from every nation, tribe, people and language, robed in the pure white of victory. They were standing before the source of strength and Jesus. They were sharing the mighty celebration, [10] as the great cry went up:

'Victory belongs to our God, who is the origin of power, and to Jesus!'

[11] All his messengers, his people and creation offered their lives, in worship before him, [12] singing:

'God's way has won! All glory, wisdom, thanks, honour, power and strength, are due to him for ever and ever. That's for sure!'

[13] Then one of the victors spoke to me.

'Do you know who these are, who are robed in victory?' he asked. 'Do you know why they conquered?'

[14] 'Sir,' I answered, 'please tell me.'

'These,' he replied, 'came through the time of great suffering. They accepted Jesus' forgiveness, and shared victoriously his self-sacrificial love. [15] That's why they live in God's presence. Every moment, they serve him in all they do, and he takes perfect care of them. [16] He satisfies their every need; nothing can break their bond with him. [17] Jesus, at the heart of power, guards them, and guides them to the springs of life. God wipes away every tear from their eyes.'

God's response to human injustice

8 [1] When Jesus broke the seventh seal, there was an awed silence. Confronted by all the injustice they had committed, humanity was dumb. Creation itself waited in silence for God's response. [2] Seven trumpeters appeared with his perfect plan: to turn earth's humans from evil. [3] All his people's petitions came before him, [4] and he heard every one.

[5] Then a new revelation was given to me. God himself would act in the dire consequences that follow from human injustice. [6] Ample warnings would be given for humanity to hear. Seven trumpeters were ready with them.

[7] At the sound of the first trumpet, the weather and climate changed. Forests and grass lands dried up, and pastures became deserts.

[8] At the sound of the second trumpet, seas became polluted, [9] and nothing could live in them. Fish were wiped out, and fishermen no longer had a living.

¹⁰ At the sound of the third trumpet rivers and springs were polluted. ¹¹ Their water became undrinkable, and many were poisoned by it.

¹² At the sound of the fourth trumpet, the pollution affected the air. The earth became a gloomy place, where midday felt like midnight. ¹³ And I saw the bird of death flying over the earth. It croaked so loud that the whole world could hear it:

'The direst consequences are still to come. Let all people on earth be warned.'

Human injustice gives people nightmares

9 ¹ At the sound of the fifth trumpet, peoples' nightmares really started. ² Earth's humans had opened the door to evil, and all hell was let loose. Unimagined horrors bubbled from the depths of perverted human minds. Darkness fell across continents. ³ The prophet's warnings were fulfilled, with plagues greater than those of Egypt. For, like Pharaoh of old, those wedded to injustice have to be forced to think again.

⁴ The physical consequences of injustice for the planet take time to appear. But other consequences for the perpetrators may come sooner. ⁵ Like a scorpion's sting they make life unbearable. ⁶ People wish they were dead, though death itself eludes them.

⁷ The path of injustice may at first appear golden. The consequences, remorseless as the emperor's armoured divisions, arrive later. ⁸ What at first seemed so alluring, ends up devouring its victims. ⁹ The day of reckoning roars in with a vengeance, ¹⁰ and the pain goes on and on. For as with the scorpion, the sting is in the tail. ¹¹ It bears all the marks of hell's ruler, the wrecker, out to destroy the Cre-

ator's work. [12] And that is but the first horror the vulture announced —there was worse to come.

[13] The sixth trumpet sounded to declare that evil must be allowed to do its worst. For only when it overreaches can its grubby deception be exposed, and every trace be rooted out. [14] So God allows what people dread most, the darkness of total barbarism. [15] As it floods across the land, it wipes out hundreds of millions. [16] Fast-moving and irresistible, [17] I saw in my dream how it spread panic and terror. [18] It wiped out whole nations, [19] and the suffering that it left behind continued for generations.

[20] But in spite of all this, people refuse to face the truth. They connive with evil's purposes, and make gods of the things they lust for. They become slaves to their own selfish desires, and are set on the road to death. [21] Like Pharaoh, they refuse to think again, and give up their addiction, adultery, killing, and theft.

John is called to be a prophet

10   [1] Then I had a blindingly brilliant vision of Jesus, victorious and merciful. Radiating light he was coming to show his people the way. [2] As ruler of all creation, the future in his hand is an open book. [3] In majestic tones, his voice spoke words that shook the heavens. [4] I was about to write them down, but they were beyond human understanding. I was told:

'Keep that secret for now. Don't write it down. When the time comes, you will understand.'

[5] Then the ruler of all creation [6] gave this complete assurance. In the name of the eternal Creator of all that is, of every kind everywhere, he decreed:

'The time has come. ⁷At the sound of the seventh trumpet the mystery of God's rule on earth will be accomplished. The great promise, foretold by his servants of old, will have been kept.'

⁸And the heavenly voice spoke to me again, saying:

'Step forward, and receive knowledge of the future, from the ruler of the earth.'

⁹So I went up to him, and asked for the book that discloses the future. He replied:

'Take it and devour it. It will be wonderful to read, but it will contain much pain for you.'

¹⁰I took the book from his hand, and devoured its contents. It was indeed wonderful to read, but it held much pain in store for me.

¹¹Then I was told:

'You must forecast again the future for many peoples, nations, languages, and rulers.'

John and the churches' prophetic role

11 ¹And I was told: 'Go to God's servants, those who are closest to him and worship him. ²Don't go to those who worship human gods, and for now persecute God's people. ³For the present, you together with those faithful, will be witnesses to my rule through your suffering. ⁴You will fulfil what I foretold, and conquer "not by might and domination, but by my Spirit". That's the way you will show that you serve the ruler of the earth. ⁵If anyone wants to harm you, your gracious words will be torment enough to them. That's how you must deal with your enemies. ⁶Your words will have the power of my great servants of old.

[7] 'Because of your witness to me, evil will do everything it can to destroy you. When you have played your part you will be killed. [8] An empire built on sexual exploitation and slavery will treat you the way it treated your ruler. [9] You won't even be allowed a decent burial. All sorts of people will want to come and gawp at your corpses. [10] The whole world will gloat over your deaths, and people will celebrate by giving each other presents. This will show just how much you trouble their consciences.

[11] 'But those who kill you are in for a colossal shock. It won't be too long before they see you resurrected! [12] Those who so hated you, will see that God himself declares you vindicated. [13] The impact of your witness will bring a change to their cities and save many lives. Because of your witness they will be filled with awe, and acknowledge what God has done. [14] But in the end those in denial, who refuse to rethink, will have to face the consequences.

God now rules the earth

[15] Then the final trumpet sounded and a great shout rang through the universe:

'Our God and his ruler now rule the earth, and his rule will last for ever!'

[16] All God's people—his appointed rulers on earth—acclaimed his power and worshipped him, [17] singing:

We thank you, all-powerful God, our ruler. You are and always were almighty. But now you have publicly taken your throne, and visibly begun to reign on earth. [18] Nations that rebelled faced the consequences, but judgement day is here for everyone. The time has come for your servants, from the greatest to the least, to share your joy. Now is the moment for your prophets,

your people, and all who revere you, to celebrate. It's time to put paid to the
destroyers of the earth.

[19] Now it was there for all to see, that God had kept his promise.
So why are there still so many problems? The mind-blowing wonder
of his ways prepared me to see the cause of all our troubles.

The Second Revelation

Why is it happening?

Evil's plan is to destroy the earth

12 ¹For centuries, faithful Jews had carried the hope of a new heaven-on-earth for all humanity—a world where humans care for the whole creation. ²After much pain, they gave birth to the promised ruler. He was the One who would crush evil, and rule the nations justly. ³For the power of evil had led every nation astray, and ruled them through its puppets. The Roman emperor and his client kings did the devil's work for him. ⁴Evil dazzled with its destructive power, and waited to destroy the promised ruler at birth.

⁵But when the child was born, evil's machinations failed to destroy him. God fulfilled his promise, and a just ruler for the nations was crowned on the cross. He rose from the dead, and ascended to rule the earth. ⁶He set his people free from evil's power, as he had planned, and met their needs so they should grow.

⁷With the Messiah's birth, the eternal struggle between good and evil reached its climax. ⁸On the cross Jesus dealt evil the fatal blow. Evil's strongest weapon, death, was turned against it. ⁹Whatever word you use for evil—the serpent, the devil, the Satan, the great deceiver of the whole world—it's what leads every human astray. But the Messiah overthrew it, and its power was left broken for ever.

¹⁰Then I heard the great sound of the universe proclaiming:

The victory, power and rule, have been won forever, by our God. All authority belongs to our ruler. The failure of the false-accuser to destroy God's people proves it. Evil, at work day and night against them, has been humili-ated. [11] *His people's victory comes through the loving power of Jesus, as they bear witness to him. For they too don't cling to life, but are ready to suffer for his sake.* [12] *So join the celebration, all his people! But let the whole earth watch out. Evil is fuming with rage against creation, because it knows that it has little time left.*

[13] Having lost its struggle against Jesus, evil's prime target is his people. [14] But they have been given the secret of liberty and are free. All their needs are met to keep them safe from the snake's wiles. [15] The false-accuser tries to drown them in a vomit of lies. It spits out a deceitful torrent, to sweep them away.

[16] But evil's lies can be seen for what they are. Its river of false-hoods fails to drown the ruler's people, [17] which infuriates it the more. It makes all out war on any who obey God's commands, and witness to the victory of Jesus. [18] Implacable, it stands ready to call in its accomplices.

Evil leads the world's rulers astray

13 [1] As I write, the bestial Roman emperor, with his client kings, runs this war on God's people. The emperor makes himself look ridiculous by calling himself the 'son of god'. [2] But his empire, like all other empires and imperial domination before it, is evil-in-spired.

[3] Once, it seemed, this empire had received a mortal blow, but it recovered. Everyone was amazed, and the nations quickly fell in line again. [4] They are, in reality, worshipping evil, because evil works through inhuman idolatrous empires. 'Who stands a chance against the emperor?' they say. 'Any resistance to his decree is futile.'

⁵ God lets big emperors with loud mouths blaspheme for a while. But their power is only granted for a limited time. ⁶ For a moment they are free to curse God and his ways, and persecute his servants. ⁷ He allows emperors to make war on Jesus' followers, and do what they like to them. After all, they have the power to treat people of any race, tribe, language or nation, that way. ⁸ And everyone in the world worships the emperor—except those following the self-sacrificial supreme ruler, Jesus. They are held secure for all time. Nothing the emperor has power to do can rob them of the life that Jesus gives.

⁹ So let those who can grasp this be prepared. ¹⁰ There are those who are going to be imprisoned; it will happen. There are those who will be put to death; that will happen too. But those faithful to Jesus will respond with positive patience, in secure hope.

Evil seems to be winning

¹¹ The emperor's little local puppets, mouthpieces of evil, strut around, puffed up like bullfrogs. ¹² Their job is to make the whole world worship the emperor and his empire. In a bad parody of Jesus, ¹³ they offer the public spectacular signs of the emperor's divinity. They even make fire fall down from the sky! They do all kinds of conjuring tricks to impress the public.

¹⁴ All this fools the credulous, and persuades them to make a statue of their 'divine' emperor. Then everyone is made to worship the image of the emperor, and make the man their god. (In a bad parody of Jesus one 'divine' emperor was murdered, then rumoured to be still alive—but he hasn't come back yet...)

¹⁵ They go so far as to make the emperor's statue seem alive and speak! So they're able to have any who won't worship it put to

death. [16] It commands everyone who worships—small and great, rich and poor, slave and citizen—to be marked on the right hand or the forehead. [17] Without that mark, or the number of its name, 666, no one is allowed to buy or sell. And if you can't buy, you can't eat.

[[18] Use your brains to decode the number 666, (which is code for 'the worst'!). In Hebrew letter-numbers it spells 'Emperor Nero', who carried out the worst imperial persecution of the Messiah's people.]

The reality is different: God is in control

14 [1] To all appearances evil seemed to be winning, but then I saw that this was an illusion. The self-sacrifice of Jesus has already won the struggle, as he overcame evil and death. Now he rules the nations, and countless numbers follow him. They bear the mark of a new character, God's gift to his servants.

[2] I heard the most beautiful divine music at full volume, filling the heavens. [3] Through Jesus' victory, they were singing to God a new song. It was a song for his people and all creation to hear. No one could learn that song, except the countless number liberated through his self-sacrifice. [4] They don't sleep around, but live purely, ready to follow Jesus anywhere he leads. They are God's vanguard among humankind, bought by Jesus with his own life. [5] They don't tell lies, and are devoid of deceit.

[6] Then I saw the great news of God's everlasting rule, being broadcast to everyone on earth. They were taking it to all nations, races, and tribes in every language. [7] Its impact was terrific:

'Face the truth, and celebrate God! The day to put right every wrong has arrived, with justice for all. Worship the One, who created the cosmos, the earth, the seas, and life itself.'

⁸ And a second great announcement went with it:

'The time for imperial domination is past. Jesus now rules! Rome, which made all the nations drunk exploiting money, power and sex, is bound to fall.'

⁹ And then a third proclamation:

'Those who worship human rulers, and go along with their unjust structures, ¹⁰ will face the consequences. It will be torture to them to be in the presence of Jesus and his followers. It will feel like fire and brimstone! ¹¹ The torment of what they've done will stay with them for ever. There's no relief, night or day, for those who choose to serve evil and its structures.'

¹² So the call to those committed to keep God's commands is to follow the faithful way of Jesus. Like him, they have to be ready to suffer for the sins of others with positive patience. ¹³ But I received this God-given promise, and I was told to write it down:

'From now on, those who give their lives to serve Jesus will enter the age to come.'

'They certainly will,' the Spirit says. 'They will be free from all their pain, and what they've lived for will go with them.'

His pure love overwhelms all evil

¹⁴ Then I looked and saw all the Messiah's people, who bear his authority on earth. They were holding to the self-sacrificial way to gather the fruits of his victory. ¹⁵ The heavenly message came loud and clear, for all to hear:

'Go out and proclaim the great news. Because the time has come, for the whole earth to become God's kingdom.'

¹⁶ And they were sent to gather his harvest from all nations.

¹⁷ After that came a further God-given message, to the reapers. ¹⁸ It came as the final call:

'Gather the harvest and follow Jesus by giving your lives. Carry the message in your lives.'

¹⁹ So the great news went out through the earth, and brought in the harvest of martyrs. Following Jesus, they themselves bore the consequence of their neighbours' injustice. ²⁰ From the ruler's and his martyrs' self-sacrifice, a river of transforming love and forgiveness flowed. It flowed deep and far enough, to make flourish the dried-up deserts of every human heart.

The Third Revelation

How will it all end up?

Evil brings about its own destruction

15 ¹Then I saw a last warning to those who choose to reject that love. I saw God's fury at injustice, as seven messengers made ready to announce the final consequence of evil's deceptions. Evil would sink under its own weight, and those who chose evil would drown in it. Injustice can't last for ever. In the end, the plagues of Egypt forced even Pharaoh to free God's people.

²And then I saw those who had come through persecution's sea of fire and splintered glass. They had been ready to die rather than deny God and worship humans. Victorious over their trials they are truly free, and share the music of heaven. ³They sing Moses' song of liberation, now transformed through Jesus:

Great and amazing is everything you do, our all-powerful God and ruler.

Your ways are just and trustworthy, ruler of the nations.

⁴*Who could not but revere and glory in your goodness, our ruler?*

You alone are pure.

All nations will bow before you, for you have shown us how to act justly.

⁵Then I saw that God had done all that he had promised to do. ⁶From the radiant, pure riches of his grace, he allows injustice to destroy itself. ⁷The seven messengers were given bowls filled with the final consequences of injustice. ⁸And even as it carries its own de-

struction, evil itself reveals God's eternal power and glory. For the consequences he affords are inevitable.

Nature itself will judge its destroyers

16 ¹ God gives us choice, and the consequences judge both ourselves, and the injustice of monstrous regimes. The story of Pharaoh tells us this. When he refused to let God's people go free, their slave-masters came out in painful sores. ² And now, when the first messenger poured out his bowl of consequences, I saw that emperor-worshippers' own bodies suffered for it.

³ After the second messenger emptied his bowl, I saw the consequences also affect the planet. For Pharaoh, the Nile became undrinkable; now I saw seas die, and every living thing in them.

⁴ As the third messenger emptied his bowl, rivers and springs of water turned the colour of blood. (This was ironic. They refused Jesus' 'life-giving blood', so their polluted rivers and springs turned the colour of blood.) ⁵ The water itself was giving its verdict on their inhumanity:

'You are pure, eternal One, and your judgement is just. ⁶ Wanting blood they spilt the blood of saints and prophets, so their water turns to "blood". (Isn't that just what they were asking for?)

⁷ Even the stones agreed:

'That's only right, our ruler, the One all-powerful God. Your decisions are just and based on the truth.'

⁸ The fourth messenger's bowl saw climates change. It brought 'the fire of judgement' from the burning sun. ⁹ In the intense heat, people cursed God.

'If he's God,' they said, 'why doesn't he stop such things?'

But they refused to rethink the way they lived, and turn to him for direction.

[10] The fifth messenger poured his bowl onto the emperor himself. General after general seized the murdered emperor's throne. Nations suffered the plunder of marching armies as civil wars erupted. People's pain was intense, [11] but it didn't make them rethink what they were living for. Yet again they cursed and blamed God for all their suffering.

[12] The sixth messenger's bowl removed the barriers to war. Fear of 'evil enemies' began to take hold of people. [13] Government, media, and local authorities, were whipped into overdrive with war propaganda. Rumours and reports twisting truth, hopped like frogs from one deception to another. [14] The demonic spirit worked overtime, dragging nations into a global war—all sides claiming to fight for Almighty God!

[[15] Hey! I hope you're following this. Keep spiritually awake to what's going on now! If you don't, you'll get confused, and you won't realise what's really happening. You will be taken in, and be part of the problem.]

[16] So everyone believes that they can solve all their problems if they destroy all the evil people.

[17] When the seventh messenger emptied his bowl into the air, that did it. [18] Everything was covered, and the result was indescribable. There had never been anything like it in the whole of human history. [19] All human structures and systems collapsed. Great idolatrous cities were ransacked, and there was total anarchy. Those who worshipped domination faced the consequence of their idolatry to the full. They got back the treatment they'd given to others. [20] Everywhere was plunged into chaos, and there was nowhere to escape.

²¹ Things too terrible for words were done, and life became unbearable.

Unjust imperial structures will collapse

17 ¹ Then I was shown the shaky nature of empire, and why it's bound to collapse. ² The empire, like a harlot, gives its favours simply for a return. Subject rulers are captivated by it, and everyone gets drunk on what they'll get out of it.

³ This led to a clearer understanding of how things are. I saw that Rome is a typical empire, ruling over a host of kingdoms. Led astray by evil, it worships its victorious armies, and proclaims its emperor a god! ⁴ As the imperial centre, the city dresses itself to seduce us with its wealth and power. Like a whore, it glitters with gold and wealth, and holds out fabulous prospects. Those sucked into its vile and filthy ways find themselves stuck, and can't get out.

⁵ Babylon of old, drunk on the blood of other nations, was the paradigm for Rome. It was the mother of all empires and their corrupt practices. ⁶ But Rome is worse, because the city is drunk on the blood of those committed to God, who has now been revealed in Jesus. Like Babylon, it is bound for a sudden fall.

⁷ I was astonished to see how absolute power could totally collapse. Then I was told that I should see through all the trappings of power. I must wake up to what was really going on. ⁸ Evil-inspired empires will rise and fall, and everyone will be over-awed by them. But those ruled by the real ruler of the earth would not be fooled by them.

⁹ People must use their brains. Rome, the city built on seven hills, will have its full number of emperors. ¹⁰ Some have already come and gone, and we have this one now. The next, when he takes

over, will have his short stay in the limelight. ([11] As for the dead emperor Nero who was supposed to come back... I'm afraid he's gone the way the rest are going.) [12] And many puppet kings in their brief day will be given thrones by the empire. [13] They will all worship the empire's domination, because their power is all owed to it.

[14] So they will all go to war against Jesus, but the love of Jesus will conquer them. For he is the ruler of rulers, and the emperor of emperors. He has called and chosen those with him, and they are faithful. [15] But Rome's empire is built on the watery foundations of subject peoples with no loyalty. They are nothing but a collection of different nations and languages with loyalty only to themselves.

[16] Evil hates its own, and destroys itself. Rome's subject rulers will turn on her, and take all her possessions. They will plunder, burn, and leave the city a ruin. [17] Only as long as it suits them, will they go along with the empire. In the end they will serve God's purposes, and fulfil his judgement on the city. [18] So that's the fate awaiting the imperial city, the trumpeted ruler over all the rulers on earth.

Their collapse will reveal God's verdict

18 [1] When I saw who was in control of everything on earth, things looked very different. The whole planet was lit up with God's glorious power. [2] I saw that appearances deceived and imperial domination was doomed. All it leaves are its evil ideas, and every form of filth and corruption. [3] All the nations are left drunk on its abuse of political and commercial power.

[4] Then another God-given word came to me:

'My people, keep clear of the imperial dream, so that you don't share in its crimes. Don't become complicit with it, or you too will face the consequences. [5] All its injustices are piled high as the sky, and God has noted every one. [6] Empires will be doubly repaid for all they do. They will be made to drink double of the poison they mix for others.

[7] 'Like all empires, Rome's pomp and orgies will turn to torment and grief. "I'll always be the world's superpower," she proclaims. "No one can overthrow me. I will never fall." [8] Such arrogance will bring its consequences on her all at once. Sick, sad and weak, she'll be plundered and reduced to nothing—that's the judgement of the One who really is powerful!

[9] 'All her subject rulers, who've enjoyed her pomp and orgies, will be in tears. They'll weep buckets when they see her downfall. [10] But they'll keep their distance, scared of suffering the same fate. "What a terrible disaster!" they'll cry. "The great imperial city, the symbol of strength itself, has suddenly fallen!"

[11] 'With the market for their goods gone, corporate dealers will be broken men. [12] Their shipments of gold, silver, jewellery, designer clothes and valuable timber, will be worthless. Their luxury goods will be valueless, along with their stocks of bronze, iron and marble. [13] There'll be no market for cinnamon, spices, myrrh, ointment, incense, wine, oil, best quality flour, corn, cattle, sheep, horses, chariots. No longer will anyone be buying human bodies—living human beings. [14] Everything that you lived for has slipped through your fingers. Your life of glamorous luxury is over for ever, never to return.

[15] 'Those who made a fortune trading with the imperial city, will do nothing to help her. Fearful of sharing her fate, they'll simply weep and bemoan their losses. [16] "What a catastrophe!" they'll wail. "Such a great city! That linen, fit for an emperor, decked with gold and precious jewels, all gone! [17] All that wealth wiped out in an hour!"

'Ship owners, travellers, sailors, and seafaring merchants, will keep well away. [18] They'll moan, "There's nowhere else we can make such money." [19] They'll tear their hair out mourning their loss, and say: "How ever could such a thing happen? Whatever can we do? Its demand for luxuries made a fortune for every ship owner, and suddenly it's all gone!"

The Fourth Revelation

The victory is won!

Celebrate God's victory!

[20] 'So let the cosmos celebrate God's justice, with all his persecuted people. He has given judgement in your favour, against imperial domination. The power-mad city that sought to destroy you has brought destruction on itself. The word of God, not the dreams of tyrants, rules the earth.'

[21] Then I saw the messenger lift a great boulder, and hurl it into the sea.

'That's what will happen to empire,' he said. 'Rome, your empire will sink like that boulder, never to rise again. [22] Your string-players, singers, flutes and trumpets will be silent for ever. Your workmen and mills will work no more. [23] Never again will the lights of your imperial city shine with joyful wedding celebrations.

'Your businessmen ruled the earth, and what did you do? With your sorcery, you exploited and led astray all the nations. So you have been judged. [24] You are found guilty, stained with the blood of prophets and saints. Rome, you merit the title, "mother of all the blood shed on the earth".'

19 [1] Then I heard the sound of the great celebration. It filled heaven and earth, like vast masses of people singing:

'Praise to our God! Freedom, glory, and power belong to him. [2] His judgements are based on the truth and are just. He has condemned the imperial domination of Rome, which corrupts the earth with its seductive idols. It will face the consequences for the murder of his servants.'

³ They repeated again:

'Praise God! The fate of the city will always be a warning to empire builders.'

⁴ And as his people and creation worshipped him, the cry rang out:

'Thank God! What he decrees is certain to happen.'

⁵ The invitation came from the throne of power itself, to great and small alike:

'Let his servants, all who revere him, give the praise due to our God.'

⁶ Then the sound surpassed the roar of the ocean and crashing thunder. Vast masses of people together hammered the message home:

'Thank God! Our ruler, the all-powerful, reigns! ⁷ Let joy flood the earth and proclaim his glory! Through the love of Jesus his people are wedded to him, and readily give their lives. ⁸ They have been given the finest design to wear, dazzling purity. For that's the look, worn by those committed to doing only good.'

⁹ Then the messenger who brought me this vision said:

'Write this down: "Those called to serve and suffer with him share his rule". That's the truth,' he added. 'It comes from God.'

¹⁰ I was so carried away by the messenger that I began to worship him.

'Look out!' he said. 'Never do that! I'm a fellow-servant with you and your comrades, who bear witness to what Jesus did. Make sure you worship God! It's from the evidence Jesus provides, that the Spirit of prophecy comes.'

How the victory was won

[11] Then I saw that Jesus overthrows evil because he was truly faithful, even to death. He ensures justice is done, because he deals with what is wrong in the right way. [12] His eyes burn through to the heart of things. He rules over all rulers, and no mind can grasp the wonder of his love. [13] He sacrificed his own life to overcome evil for us. In him, God's words and actions are one. [14] All who battle against evil with him follow his way of purity, victorious through suffering.

[15] His words cut to the core, destroying the nations' idolatry. He rules and breaks their rebellion with his love. In almighty God's fury at humans' injustice, he has taken on himself the consequences due to them. [16] His title, 'King of Kings' and 'Ruler of Rulers', is written in his own blood.

[17] And I saw the glorious day being broadcast to all the nations under the heavens:

'You're invited! Come in and share God's great feast. [18] Rule over rulers, generals and armies; over the powerful, citizens, slaves, small and great alike.'

[19] The call stung emperors and 'little emperors' into action across the globe. They gathered all their forces to make war on Jesus and his followers. [20] But in spite of all its lies and propaganda, evil is bound to lose. It may trick people to collude with it, and drive people to conform. But the empire and its idolatry, along with its collaborators, will come to a sticky end. [21] What remains of it will melt away at the news of Jesus' victory. And all the nations will share in the great celebration.

20 ¹I saw that Jesus has the power to deal with evil forever, ²for he has defeated it. Whatever guise evil may take, he has limited its power to harm for as long as needed. ³His victory so weakened it, that it can never abort God's purposes for the nations. Before the final resurrection, the last traces of it will be exposed for complete removal.

Judgement day—death itself is destroyed

⁴Then I saw that judgement is already taking place. For the judges condemning the martyrs are in reality condemning themselves. With the resurrection of Jesus 'the resurrection age' began, and the martyrs act—as they will after the final resurrection—with the pure selfless love of the resurrected. They already live like the resurrected, and bear witness to the victory of Jesus as God's word. They are not overcome by pressure to serve human domination and worship human idols. They refuse to conform to subhuman practices, and even now live and reign with him.

⁵The rest of humanity do not live like resurrected people. So they will have to wait for their verdict until the final resurrection. ⁶But those committed to Jesus, who now share the fruit of his resurrection, are privileged. They rule with him, as channels of his love, for as long as this age lasts. They know that eternal death will not be able to touch them.

⁷In the end every last hint of evil will be exposed and dealt with. ⁸But evil will not give up without a fight. Masses of people led astray and wedded to evil will emerge in every corner of the earth. They will bulldoze the nations to follow their way, and the powers of destruction will do their worst. ⁹They will use any means to crush those

committed to a society built on pure love. But the fire of the Spirit will swallow them up. [10] Every evil which damaged and destroyed will join imperial domination and deception in oblivion.

[11] Then I saw the author of power and purity take his judgement seat. Before him even the universe itself, besmirched by evil, was found wanting. [12] I saw the dead, from the highest to the lowest, up before the seat of Judgement. Their whole lives were open to him, and all were judged by what they had lived for. And the book was opened, recording those who had chosen life.

[13] All the dead were there, no matter how they died. All were to be judged in the same way, by what they had lived for. [14] Death lost all its victims, and was itself judged. Death itself was condemned to death. [15] There was now no future left for anyone whose choice was to follow evil.

The new heavens and earth are born

21 [1] I saw the new universe, with all earth's wrongs put right; where evil no longer existed. [2] I saw the God-given new society arriving, the kingdom of heaven coming on earth. It was breathtaking in its beauty, for the love of God ruled all.

[3] I heard the great announcement:

Open your eyes! God is at home among his people!

He's going to live with humans. They will be his people, and he will be their God; God-with-them. [4] *He will wipe away all their tears. There will be no more death, no more mourning, no more sadness, no more pain. The world of the past is over.*

[5] Then the Creator of all declared:

'Look! I am making newness itself new! Put it in writing. You can trust that it is so, because I tell the truth.'

⁶ And he added,

'Everything I say is no sooner said than done. I am the author and the goal of life, the beginning and end of everything. I will give the new life freely to anyone who seeks it. ⁷ Those martyred for bearing witness to me, will inherit it. I will be their God, and they will be my children.

⁸ 'But all deceivers of every kind—the untrustworthy, depraved, murderers, sex-worshippers, occultists—serve the lie. For them and any who act against their conscience, the future is bleak. Those who worship people and things are bound to suffer the consequences. They destroy their own future.'

⁹ I heard one of those who first announced God's final liberating response to evil, say to me:

'Come and see this. I'll show you the church obedient to the self-denying Jesus.'

A larger vision of God's gift

¹⁰ Then he enlarged my vision to see the new, wondrous society, God's gift to the earth. It was founded on Jesus' self-sacrifice, ¹¹ and its glory came from following him. It shone crystal-clear like a priceless treasure. ¹² Free from fear, it lay open for all God's people to enter. Everything was there ready for them. ¹³ God welcomed them from everywhere, north, south, east and west. ¹⁴ It was founded by those who first proclaimed the great news of Jesus' rule.

¹⁵ This was the New Jerusalem, foretold by God's servants of old. ¹⁶ It is the place where God makes his home. It is broad and

wide enough to include the whole world. [17] All his people live there in perfect security, [18] and its protection is beyond price. It is a society, built on what is most valuable, and it is totally transparent. [19] Its foundations have indescribable worth and beauty, [20] and fulfil all the promises in the Bible. [21] It is worth more than anything, to enter it. It has no hidden agendas, and is open for all to see, pure and priceless.

[22] There is no temple. Its temple is the earth's ruler, Almighty God and the self-sacrificial Jesus. [23] It needs no sun or moon to light its ways. The glory of God and the self-denying love of Jesus are its light. [24] The nations will live by its light, with the world-rulers' values transformed by it. [25] It is open all day long, to everyone, and there is no night. [26] The best the nations have to give will be brought into it. [27] There is no pollution, nothing ugly, nothing deceptive, and everyone lives overflowing with life, because of Jesus.

22 [1] My guide showed me the love of God in Jesus flowing from the heart of the city. This great river of life, sparkling like crystal, [2] fed the life of the city. Its fruits of peace, unity and joy, heal the wounds of the nations. [3] All the things that cursed humanity, are gone.

His servants no longer fall prey to lesser aims, but serve God and Jesus alone. [4] They will see him face to face and share his purity and love. [5] Darkness, the realm of evil, will be no more; light of sun and lamps no longer needed. For God will rule over them for ever, and his glorious presence will radiate their light.

The time for all this to happen is now!

[6] God's messenger explained to me:

'What you have heard is real,' he said, 'and you can trust it. It is the ruler, God, who inspires true prophets, who has revealed this for his servants. It is already in process and bound to happen. ⁷Use your eyes! It's already coming. His persecuted people, who take on board what this prophetic book says, will share it.'

⁸I, John, am the one who heard and saw these things. I was again overwhelmed and began to worship the messenger, who had shown them to me. ⁹He reacted with horror:

'Watch out! What do you think you're doing? I'm just a fellow-servant, like you and your brother prophets, and those who put this into practice. Make sure it's God you're worshipping.'

¹⁰And he added this:

'Don't keep these prophecies secret, because now is the time for them. ¹¹People can choose to go on being unjust, and the filthy can choose to go on polluting. Or people may choose to act justly. They have the chance to do things God's way, with no selfish motives and agendas. ¹²But there is little time left to choose, and the choice is crucial. Enter the new age of a just society, or go down with the old corrupt one. For everyone will face the consequences of what they choose to live for.

So take it all on board!

¹³'I am what life's all about, the beginning and goal of everything. ¹⁴Those who accept my forgiveness and are ready to die for me, I empower with new life. They are free, and a new earth lies open before them. ¹⁵Those who serve man-made gods—tricksters, sex-corrupters, murderers, idolaters loving and pushing the lie—won't get it.

¹⁶'All this is given to you, to give to the churches. I, Jesus, confirm it to you, and I am the Ruler promised in the scriptures. I am the

dawn of the age to come. [17] God's Spirit and his people invite you to find life. Come and get it! Let everyone who hears the news pass on the invitation. Come and get it! Everyone who is looking for something real will find it. Anyone who wants to discover what life's all about can do so—and it's free!

[18] 'But I have to warn everyone who reads these prophecies, against adding "ifs" and "buts". If you do, you'll be back with the consequences. [19] If anyone waters down the prophecies in this book, they will miss out. The overflowing riches of real living will always be a mystery to them. They will never receive the life described in this book.'

[20] The One who confirms these things says:

'It really is all now in process.'

So that's it. Jesus, our ruler, let your work be completed.

[21] May the grace of Jesus, the earth's ruler, be with all. May God let it so be.

How to unpack Revelation

Translators must remember...

To find the everyday meaning of John's words, there are always seven things to keep in mind.

1. John's is an apocalyptic writing.

We must remind ourselves that prophets like John used an 'apocalyptic' form, a 'cryptic disclosure of things which otherwise remain hidden'. (Jesus also used this form at times—for example, in the parable of the sower.) So Revelation is not written in 'plain English', or rather 'plain Greek', but using symbols. These symbols are not meant to be taken 'literally'. What we have to look for is what they represent, and what they indicate.

2. Revelation uses numbers as code

Numbers in Revelation were used as code.

- 1 stands for the One God.
- 2 is the number of witnesses required in a court of law to prove that something is true.
- 3 is code for God in the form of the Holy Trinity: Father, Son and Holy Spirit.
- 4 calls up the four winds and 'the four corners of the earth', and is code for the earth.
- 5 and 10 (the number of fingers on one and both hands) are round numbers.
- 6 is bad news, because it falls short of 7.

• 7 stands for completion or perfection.
• 8 is one more than 7 and so adds to perfection.

[Note: The Hebrew way of thinking and expression lies behind the whole book. In Hebrew the way 'more' and 'most' are expressed is by doubling or trebling the word. So God is 'Holy, holy, holy', 'the most holy'. Numbers work in the same way: as 8 adds to perfection. 88 is even better and 888 is best —in Greek letter-numbers in fact 'Jesus' adds up to spell 888!]

• 12 represents the 12 apostles Jesus sent out. It also represents the 12 tribes of Jews, brought about through the work of the apostles, which transformed by Christ now include both Jews and Gentiles.
• 24 represents the 12 apostles and 12 tribes of the people of God, the church together.
• 1,000 represents a vast number.
• 144,000 is the 12 apostles times the 12 tribes of God's people times 1,000 = 'a number, no one can count'.

3. Allusions to scripture are key

Most of us today are unfamiliar with the Bible's 'Old Testament', the Hebrew scriptures. But without such knowledge, Revelation is a closed book to us. John wrote in Greek, but his world-view is that of the Hebrew scriptures. He has these books in mind all the time, and alludes to many different passages in them. On average there are nearly two allusions to passages in them in every verse!

These allusions provide keys to some of the meaning for the reader. They also shout through all his book: 'this is the fulfilment of all that the scriptures say'. They tell us: 'this is the next stage in the story of what the earth was created for. It charts the continuous and final stage of our journey'.

For instance, John's allusions call up and follow the story told in the book of Exodus:

God's people in slavery are liberated through the plagues—they escape through the Red Sea where their enemies are drowned—on the far shore they sing the song of Moses' victory—but then they worship the golden calf—a great struggle to build God's dwelling place ensues until—finally, God comes to dwell with his people.

This all now has deeper meaning in the light of Jesus. John also follows sequences given by the prophets Ezekiel, Zechariah, Daniel, Isaiah, and Jeremiah. Psalms are another favourite source for him.

4. Nuances were different 2,000 years ago

We must also remember that words imply different things in different world-views. John had a Hebrew mindset, and now sees everything transformed through the eyes of Jesus. So for John, 'justice' is transformative justice. It is not our common idea of 'an eye for an eye', but of healing what is wrong.

This means that John's language is often no longer politically correct. He writes in a way that sounds highly militaristic! He sees a stark divide between good and evil, and permanent war between them. But all this is of course about spiritual warfare. He is talking about the eternal struggle between good and evil in each human heart.

5. John's idea of heaven is not 20th century

For many people today heaven may be thought of as a place somewhere in outer space. But this was not a Jewish idea. For Jews heaven and earth were joined together in the temple in Jerusalem. God's special 'presence' was there in the holy of holies at the heart of the temple, and God was fully engaged in history. As the Prophet Isaiah put it, 'he rolled up his sleeves' ready to get his hands dirty.

So heaven was not a distant place but rather, we might say, a different dimension. From ancient times prophets were invited into heaven, to be told the future. When the same invitation came to John it was a simple step to go there.

Heaven was not seen as the final destination for humans. It was only thought of as a temporary 'resting place' until the day of resurrection. When that day arrived, earth and heaven would be one, in a renewed earth and heaven together.

6. John knows his churches' situations

John uses local angles to deal with common issues. The people John writes to face many challenges, and John shows detailed knowledge of them. Some of these are quite clear, and bring to life his friends' situation. But sometimes, because of our limited knowledge, it is unclear. Then we have to make a judgement, and choose what best fits John's mindset and the whole story.

7. We do not know everything!

Sometimes too, because of our limited knowledge, a passage of the text is unclear, and we cannot be certain what John is referring to. Then again, we have to make a judgement, and choose what best fits John's mindset and the whole story.

Sample notes on the text

To explain a little of what lies behind the translation

Heading numbers are the Bible chapter numbers. Small numbers give the verses.

The Introduction

1

[1] *the earth's ruler*, literally, 'Christ', in Hebrew 'Messiah', which means '(God's) anointed (King)' = 'God's appointed King'. We must keep in mind that kings were absolute rulers, regarded as the nation itself. The prophecy in Psalm 2:8 states that the 'Son' (a descendant) of King David will be ruler over the nations. So if Jesus is the Christ, he fulfils this role. The whole Psalm is constantly in John's mind. He is saying that this Psalm is 'fulfilled' in the present earthly reality.

[2] *supreme ruler*, literally, 'Christ' (see verse 1) as spelt out in 1 Timothy 6:15.

[4] *to every*, literally, 7, because 7 is the code for 'complete'. While these letters have special relevance to those named, they are intended for the entire church, and for all time. The whole book is a letter to the whole church.

[7] *those who killed him*, simply fulfils the prophecy of Zechariah 12.10, and is not (as it has been used for) anti-Semitic triumphalism. (Anyway, it was the Romans who killed Jesus, as John is to point out.) It emphasizes that everyone will recognise him, no one will be excluded.

[8] *the beginning and goal*, literally in Greek 'alpha and omega', the first and last letters of the Greek alphabet. This emphasizes again that this *is* the present earthly reality.

[9] *the bible promised suffering*. See the prophecy of Isaiah 53. The Messiah's followers follow him, suffering for his sake—to demonstrate and bring about his rule on earth. This is also for the sake of others, to offer them the Messiah's liberation.

[10] *one Sunday*, literally, 'the Lord's day'. The resurrection of Jesus was the first day of new creation, the resurrection age, now in process. For the Messiah's followers it changed their special weekly celebration day from the Sabbath, (Saturday), to Sunday.

[13] *Jesus... victorious*, literally, 'the son of man' who in Daniel 7:13 symbolises the 'true Jews', those who were wholly committed to God. In Daniel's prophetic judgement scene, God promises victory over the beast, their evil enemy, to the wholly committed. Jesus was the only one wholly committed to God, so can claim to be the 'true Jews', 'the Son of Man'. He claimed the victory over evil, the real enemy, (see his parable, Luke 11:20-22). So to call Jesus the 'son of man' is to call up the whole victorious judgement scene of Daniel 7.

giving them courage, literally, 'a golden sash'. John is calling up the whole picture of Daniel 10:5-19, which climaxes with the Son of Man —now seen as Jesus—giving him courage. In the same way Jesus is giving courage to his churches.

[14] *God's wisdom*, literally, 'hair white as snow'. This image is again taken from Daniel 7. Age was greatly respected as bringing wisdom. Thus Daniel 7:9 symbolises God with the wisdom of the ages.

[16] *words cutting sharper than a two-edged sword*. Jesus is seen as 'the servant', described in Isaiah chapters 40-55. The sword in Revelation stands for God's word, taken from the image in Isaiah 49:2.

[17] *look on God and live.* See the statement in Exodus 33:20. This is the reason for him falling 'like a dead man at his feet'.

2

All the letters carry references to the local context. Something of that context has been included in the text to make the references clear. Here are just two examples taken from the first and last churches mentioned.

[7] At Ephesus, the great temple of Diana had a garden and tree as described. It is for this reason that John gives the alternative offer of a garden with a tree of life. It tells us what God's original purpose was for that tree in the Garden of Eden, Genesis 3:22. This underlines that God's plan from the beginning of eternal life, is being fulfilled, and will be completed in the end.

3

[15] The river Lycus dries up in summer. But water flowed to the town from snow-capped Mt Cadmus. In the summer heat it was tepid by the time it reached the town. An alternative aqueduct also brought hot water to the town from natural springs to the north. This too had become tepid by the time it arrived at Laodicea. So John's charge against the church there is that its commitment to the Messiah has also become 'tepid'.

Laodicea was a famously wealthy city, strategically placed on the main north-south, east-west crossroads. It produced much sought after black wool from its rare black sheep. It also had a medical school, and manufactured a much sought after eye ointment.

All this background information is used in the way John writes to the church there, and so is included in the text.

The First Revelation

What is happening?

What is going to happen?

4

[1] *earth's operations centre*, literally, 'heaven'. Heaven was not the place to stay for ever after death. It was a temporary resting place before final, 'soul' (life) and body resurrection into the new earth and heaven. God is acting in history, and heaven is the 'centre' from where he directs the forces of good on earth—in the struggle between good and evil in the human heart. What is happening on earth is 'reflected' in heaven, as God works out the fulfilment of his plan for the whole of creation.

[3] *mercy*, literally 'rainbow'. The rainbow was the sign of God's mercy for the earth. It fulfils God's promise, signed by a rainbow, in Genesis 9:15.

[4] *those with true humanity*. The 24 elders represent the first 12 apostles that Jesus appointed. They are joined by the renewed 12 tribes of 'Israel', the church of both Jews and Gentiles together. They are now called to be the people of God. The crucifixion of Jesus climaxed

the inhumanity that had taken over the earth. Jesus brought true humanity, the image of God in Genesis 1:27, back on earth. The followers of the Messiah are not to be run by their old nature. They are to be transformed and act with true humanity, according to the plan of God.

[6, 7] *evil lay powerless*, literally 'sea of glass'. To the Hebrew mind the sea was an evil place, from which monsters emerge, see Daniel 7:2-3. Before God the sea is made solid, unmoving, unable to harm.

wild and domestic, literally, '... lion... ox...' The 'creatures' represent wild and domestic animals, birds, and spiritually-deprived humans, not 'truly human' and consciously ruled by God.

[10] *wills*, literally, 'crowns'. From their royal role, Exodus 19:6, (see Before we begin - Alice in Wonderland). These are the real crowned rulers on earth in God's eyes, not the human parodies of them. They are to rule the earth God's way.

5

[1] *unbreakable seals*, literally, 'sealed with seven seals.' 7, of course, means that it is perfectly sealed. John is alluding in this verse to Ezekiel 2:10. It tells us that his commission to prophesy the future is in line with that of the prophet Ezekiel. So John follows the order in Ezekiel's prophecy.

[2] *everywhere*, literally 'a great voice', one loud enough for all the world to hear.

[5] *One long promised*, literally, 'root of David'. Jesus was a descendant, (by legal adoption,) of King David, the revered founder of the Jewish kingdom. David was promised, in 2 Samuel 7:12, that a descendant of his would set up his rule for ever.

has the strength of a lion, literally, 'lion from the tribe of Judah.' Jesus, like David, was descended from the patriarch Judah, who was said to be like a lion in Genesis 49:9.

triumphed. Jesus turns the word 'triumph' on its head. He did not think the enemy was 'the evil people', as everyone else did. He saw the enemy as 'the Satan', 'the great deceiver' of Job 1, 'the devil', 'evil itself'. His triumph over it was, of course, on the cross! (There evil did its worst. First, it lost the struggle to turn him back from following God's plan for the Messiah. Then it lost the struggle to get him to hate his 'enemies' and curse his torturers, but he forgave them.)

[6] *a Lamb... it was Jesus.* Because Jesus, God's servant, is seen as the lamb 'led to the slaughter' in Isaiah 53:7, to heal all humanity.

crucified and resurrected, literally, 'slain and standing'(!). The Greek verb 'to stand' can mean both 'standing' and 'resurrected'.

all-powerful, literally, '7 horns', make him invincible, (horns symbolise weapons, 7 perfect).

all-seeing, literally, '7 eyes'. 7 for complete sight, seeing everything.

the perfect Spirit, literally, '7 spirits', taken from Isaiah 11:2. According to the prophet Joel 2:28, when God's rule is set up on earth God's Spirit will be available to everyone.

[11-14] All creatures on earth join in praising God, by reflecting his creative nature. But only humans offer him rational worship.

6

The future is now revealed to John. The first symbols he sees suggest very strongly human activity, and its consequences.

The first four prophecies, and the last three prophecies, are similar. This tells us that in spite of appearances, 3, code for God the Trinity is still in control over 4, code for the earth.

[1] *Jesus*, literally 'the lamb', broke the first seal. It is through Jesus that we see the future differently. Each of the, literally, 'four living creatures' of chapter 4:7, announces one of the consequences of human action. The first was, literally, 'like a lion', hence the king of the jungle. These are not prophecies of a particular happening, but are prophecies of the future in general.

[2] *men wanting to be King... out to conquer*, literally, 'white horse... A crown was given to him.' White is the colour of victory, and the crown is here the imperial crown that dominates. This is not about any specific empire, but about all imperial domination, large or small.

exploiting power, literally, 'to further his victories.' 'The four horsemen of the Apocalypse', as they are called, represent four kinds of human behaviour. The first covers every sort of empire building by those who have power. The literal text has a horseman with 'a bow'. This bow was seen as the supreme weapon of the day. It was developed by the Parthian Empire, just over the border, for their cavalry. They were feared as a constant threat.

[5] *economic crashes*, literally, 'black horse'.

corruption, literally, 'a pair of scales in his hand'. In this context the allusion to 'scales' calls up Hosea 12:7, 'A trader in whose hands are false scales loves to oppress'; and also Amos 8:4,5 'you bring to ruin the poor... and practise deceit with false scales.'

[6] *The price was always to be paid by the poor's intense suffering'*, literally, 'a day's pay for a quart of wheat'. Economic crashes are bad news for the poor. The price of their staple foods (wheat and barley) rockets.

The luxury goods of the rich are untouched, literally, 'don't damage the oil and wine'. These are expensive essentials for those with money, and are seen as symbols of the wealthy. Nothing can ever be allowed to harm the lifestyle of the rich.

¹²⁻¹⁷ *Nations were shaken to pieces*, literally, 'a great earthquake.' This uses language in the way today we speak of 'earth-shaking' events. The final verses of the chapter are a picture of the complete collapse of society. The bible uses similar phrases elsewhere such as 'the sun going dark', the 'moon turning to blood', and 'stars going out'. (See for example Isaiah 13:10.)

7

People who worshipped the Roman emperor were given a 'seal' or 'mark' on their forehead or hand. This showed to everyone in the market place that they had worshipped Caesar as a god.

John picks up the idea. The followers of the Messiah are also sealed with a mark. It is an invisible mark, the character of the Messiah written on their foreheads. It marks them out as the 'conquerors', over all the suffering they have to undergo.

As they are the renewed 12 tribes of God's people, John ensures that no one is forgotten. The literal text symbolises this by giving complete lists of the 12 ancient Hebrew tribes.

⁴ *the apostles... multiplied past counting*, literally, '144,000'. This represents the 12 apostles times the 12 tribes, (those who believe through their word,) times 1,000. Here it is the 'countless number', literally, 'that no man can number', of verse 9.

[12] *That is assured!* Literally, 'Amen!' It is a Hebrew word meaning 'God strengthen it'.

8

The trumpeters—who announce God's response to people's inhumanity—call up the plagues of Egypt. These had forced the Pharaoh to free the people of God from slavery in Egypt. The trumpets echo the plagues. They show that God's purpose now is to free the whole world from slavery to evil. They are symbolic, but we might say that God shows people the consequence of their actions on the environment. This may bring people to their senses, and help free them from the power of evil. It's important to remember that God's only concern is the good of humanity.

The consequences are grouped, the first 4 being similar, then 3 others rather different. (As was also the case with the 7 seals.) 4 represents the earth, and 3 represents God, the holy Trinity, ruler of the earth. This grouping tells us again that God is still in control of the earth, in spite of appearances.

[5] *a further revelation*, literally, 'thunder, rumblings, lightning, earthquake...' These were the dramatic background to God's revelation to Moses on Mount Sinai. They indicate that God is about to give a new revelation.

[7] *climate changed*, literally, 'a third of the trees and grass were burned up.' But we must remember all the time that John is writing symbolically.

9

[2] *all hell*, literally, 'bottomless pit'. In Greek mythology, the place where the dead are kept is called Hades. There was a place below Hades for particularly bad people. Evil is consigned to the lowest place, described here literally as 'the abyss'. Jesus said that evil intentions come from within the human heart. This whole vision is conjured up from Joel 1. (See especially Joel 1:4.)

[11] *the wrecker*, literally, 'the destroyer'. Evil spreads the idea that evil is 'creative' and 'fun', and those doing anything good are 'kill joys'. The truth is rather different. John describes evil literally as 'the King of Destruction'. To emphasise the point he writes it in Hebrew, and also in Greek (where it might be better translated 'the murderer').

[14] *total barbarism*, literally, 'messengers at... river Euphrates'. The Euphrates was the boundary of Parthia. There was constant dread of a great Parthian (Persian) army from the east pouring in to overrun them. The Parthians had horsemen who carried a bow, (found in the literal translation at 6:2.) It was seen as the nuclear weapon of the day. This threat gave people nightmares. It was seen as a further fulfilment of the warnings of the prophet Joel 2:4 and following verses, which describe being overrun by armies.

10

John's book begins with him being announced as a prophet. His call to prophesy is now recounted in detail. This follows the pattern of Isaiah 6:1-13. Tracking the prophets in this way shows subliminally that John is their present-day equivalent. It continuously affirms that everything he is saying is in line with God's purposes from the beginning. Just as there was a dramatic pause before the seventh seal, so there is a dramatic pause before the seventh trumpet.

[1] *Jesus*, literally, 'cloud... rainbow... sun... pillars of fire'. Because Jesus fits the description in the vision which John saw at the start. Clouds, rainbow, pillars of fire, are all symbols of divinity.

[4] *Keep that secret for now*, because he follows the prophet Daniel 12:4. The meaning of Daniel's prophecy was not to be known until the time of its fulfilment in Jesus. So for the moment John is to keep this prophecy secret, until the final resurrection.

11

[1] *God's servants*, literally, 'temple of God', replacing the old temple in Jerusalem. The Messiah's followers have now become God's temple, the place where God's Holy Spirit lives, see 1 Corinthians 6:19. John here calls up Ezekiel's vision of the temple following the resurrection. John sees that age, the resurrection age, begun on the morning of Jesus' resurrection. His resurrection foreshadows the general resurrection which must follow, as St Paul explains in 1 Corinthians 15.

[3] *Together with those faithful*, literally, 'two witnesses.' Two witnesses are required in law to prove something is true. Here John is following Zechariah 4:3, 13-14. He together with the church is fulfilling the role of two anointed prophets.

[4] *not by might...* Like Jesus, when John refers to the scriptures, he has the whole context in mind. Zechariah 4:6 tells us how the two witnesses are to be victorious.

[6] *the power of...*, literally, 'shut the sky... turn into blood'. Having two witnesses proves that their evidence is the truth. As prophets they will be as powerful as the two greatest prophets of old, Elijah and

Moses. Elijah because he caused there to be no rain, and Moses because he turned water to blood.

[8] *empire*, literally, 'Sodom and Egypt'. Sodom was a notorious centre of sexual exploitation, and Egypt of Israel's slavery. Together they now symbolise the Roman Empire that rules them, which crucified Jesus. Its sexual exploitation is like the city of Sodom. Like the Egypt of Pharaoh, it now tries to destroy God's people.

[12] *vindicated*, literally, 'went up in a cloud.' John calls up Daniel 7:13. There the metaphor of 'coming with clouds'—or rather 'going(!)' from our point of view, the Hebrew and Greek can be either—means 'vindicated by God'.

[17] *visibly begun to reign on earth.* On the cross, for all the world to see, his title in three languages.

The Second Revelation

Why is it happening?

12

Up till now, events may appear quite haphazard. Here, evil is at last exposed as itself, the cause of what's going wrong. It makes a dramatic entry in pantomime style, showing how ridiculous it is—but dangerous.

[1] *faithful Jews*, literally, a 'woman' with '12 stars', 12 being code for the tribes of Israel. It is 'Israel' that gives birth to the Messiah.

care for the whole creation, literally, 'crown' (see Before we begin -
Alice in Wonderland)). They are called to be the 'rulers' over all creation, literally 'sun and moon'.

² *much pain*. Literally, 'birth pangs'. The true Jews who held faithful
to God through all their suffering 'gave birth' to the Messiah.

⁵ *evil's machinations failed*, literally 'snatched away to God'. King Herod
killed all the babies in Bethlehem in a failed attempt to kill the baby
Jesus.

⁷ *the eternal struggle*, literally, 'war in heaven'. A literal translation describes the battle as in heaven, but we discover (in verse 11) that this
reflects the battle won on earth. It is the story of Jesus' victory, and
the victory of those who follow in his footsteps.

¹⁶ *river of falsehoods*, literally 'river the dragon poured...' This is the
situation of the people John writes to. They are subjected to a torrent
of lies told about them by the imperial government and their neighbours.

13

John has to deal with the situation facing the churches in the
Roman Empire. They were being persecuted. Those doing the actual
persecuting were local officials, who sought to curry favour with the
emperor.

¹ *Roman emperor*, literally 'beast rising out of the sea'. The emperor
and his army initially came across the sea to conquer the Jews. For
the Jews the sea was also a place from which bad things came.

² *a paradigm of all empires*, literally, 'leopard, bear, lion.' John combines
the symbols of the previous empires, Babylonians, Persians, Greeks,
that had ruled the Jews, see Daniel 7:3-7.

[3] *this empire... a mortal blow*, literally, 'One of its heads... death blow'. This is another reference to the strange rumours about the emperor Nero, murdered in 68 AD. His murder was followed within a year by three revolutions in succession, as generals one after another seized the imperial crown. The empire was stabilised again by the last of these, Vespasian.

[12] *just a parody of Jesus*, literally, 'whose mortal wound has been healed'. That is, come alive from the dead. John is playing on the rumour that the murdered Emperor Nero was still somehow alive somewhere.

[18] *Use your brains to decode... 666.* You have to know Hebrew! The letters of Emperor Nero's name written in Hebrew, then used as Hebrew numbers, add up to 666! That's also, of course, the code for 'worst', (see How to unpack Revelation, 2 -Revelation uses numbers as code). Nero was guilty of the most depraved horrific murders of Christians. He was the emperor who initiated imperial persecution.

14

[1] *The self-sacrifice of Jesus*, literally, 'lamb standing on Mount Zion.' Putting the thoughts and symbol of Isaiah 53 together with Psalm 2. The servant, the Messiah, is a lamb for sacrifice in Isaiah 53. Mount Zion is Jerusalem in Psalm 2. 'Standing' has the meaning 'resurrected' (see John 20:19). 'Rule the nations' is called up from Psalm 2, because it says that God has 'set his King on Zion' to rule over the nations of the earth.

[4] *They are his pure, elite legions*, literally, 'not defiled... with women'. If war was justified in ancient Israel it was holy, so it required purity before any battle, see Deuteronomy 23:9, 10; 1 Samuel 21:5. Those John is writing to are elite warriors, always ready for spiritual bat-

tle. Jesus' constant command is 'Follow me'. They have to be ready to suffer any moment, and to die if necessary. This vast host is just the vanguard, literally the 'first fruits', which were offered to God in the temple. It's an assertion of a different society.

[10] *will face the consequence*, literally 'drink the wine of God's wrath'. God's 'wrath' is his fury at evil, which is destroying his creation. It is not wrath against people. It is to be seen on earth in the consequences brought about by human agency. The tragic consequences are not directed against people, but for their good.

[11] *The torment...*, literally, 'the smoke of their torment goes up forever and ever'. Their self-inflicted torture will of course come from their consciences for their evil deeds.

[14] *Jesus ruling the whole earth from the cross*, literally, 'the Son of Man', taken from Daniel 7. He is now the victorious ruler over all nations.

self-sacrificial way, literally 'sickle'. The sickle he holds is a symbol for the Cross, which is Jesus' way of gathering in the harvest of the nations.

[15] *the time has come, for the whole earth to enter into God's kingdom*, literally 'the harvest of the earth is fully ripe'. Because only after the Jews have done the job of setting up God's rule on earth, can all nations enter it, (that was without first becoming Jews).

[19] *Following Jesus* (self-sacrifice), literally, 'winepress of the wrath of God'. The cross shows God's fury at evil's destruction of his creation. It is the extent to which God will go for the sake of 'his children'.

river of transforming love, literally, 'blood flowed out... 200 miles'. John picks up the vision of the healing river flowing out from beneath the new temple, in Ezekiel 47:1. He turns it into a river of blood: the sacrifice by Jesus of his own blood, his own life, now joined by that of his followers.

The Third Revelation

How will it all end up?

15

[1] *Evil would sink... God's fury...*, literally, 'portent... seven plagues... the wrath...' People, who have refused to change their behaviour, will have to face the consequences of their actions. In the end there is no more that God can do. John makes this clear by again echoing Pharaoh of old, and the plagues of Egypt.

[2] *persecution's sea of fire*, literally, 'a sea of glass mixed with fire'. The sea symbolises the realm of evil, now turned to glass, and so made powerless, see 4:6. Here, John calls up the Jews escaping from Egypt to freedom through the Red Sea. So now those suffering martyrdom by following Jesus, are set free from slavery.

[3] After going through the Red Sea, the people saw the pursuing army drowned trying to follow them. The people were now finally free, and they sang Moses' song of victory. John echoes this story as the story of Messiah's martyrs. Through their martyrdom they demonstrate that God now rules the nations.

[7] *God's fury at injustice*, literally 'the wrath of God'. However this idea may be understood elsewhere, for John its meaning is wholly transformed by Jesus. The cross is the self-sacrificial final victory of Jesus over evil. It demonstrates the boundless fury of God at the destruction of his creation.

16

In this chapter, John calls up the book of Leviticus 26:21, 'if you will not obey me, I will plague you sevenfold for your sins... If by these things you are not turned to me'—then you will end up in exile from me. The whole chapter is telling us: if you choose evil, you lose knowledge of God and face catastrophe.

John is now bringing out the finality of the story of the plagues of Egypt. As always, we must remember that his language is symbolic. It is telling us that nature itself—the earth, sea, rivers and sun—judges those responsible for looking after it. For God's plan was that people 'made in his image' would care for creation. When instead they join in damaging it, they will face the consequences.

[10] *the emperor himself*, literally, 'on the throne of the beast'. This is a direct attack on imperialism itself. In real life terms it is telling us that imperialism will collapse under its own weight.

[11] John has been re-telling the story of Daniel 7:25-27, in the light of the people's experience. He is in the process of declaring that sovereignty will be taken away from Rome's imperial domination. 'Rule' over all the nations will in future be given to the people of God. John claims Jesus now rules, and does so through those who follow him.

17

[1] *shaky nature of empire*, literally, 'whore seated on many waters.' John's symbol of the whore is not one of trafficked girls. She is the high-class prostitute by choice, out to make a fortune. The symbol comes from the prophet Hosea 2:5, who used it as a metaphor for chasing idols. John sees Rome's idolatrous empire thriving on sex indulgence. Like sexual fantasy the empire lured peoples in—only to

find they had to drink its economic and social oppression. Once in they are stuck and can't get out. The 'whore', the empire, is a parody of 'the bride'. His book is about the Creator and his creation, Genesis 1:1. It is about the bridegroom, God, (see Isaiah 62:5,) and his people, his bride. In Revelation 21:2 the bride, Israel, has now become the church.

[2] *everyone gets drunk on what they'll get out of it*, literally, 'with the wine of fornication, the earth's inhabitants have become drunk.' John is calling up Jeremiah 51:7, 'Babylon has been a golden cup, intoxicating all the earth. The nations have drunk of her wine; therefore the nations are going mad.' Babylon was the great empire that destroyed the temple and Jerusalem, and carried the Jews away captive. John sees it as the paradigm of all empires. So it applies equally to Rome, the empire that rules John's world.

[4] *wealth and power*, literally, 'purple and scarlet.' Purple was the imperial colour. Scarlet denotes Rome, the power of the 'scarlet woman'.

[7] *complete power*, literally '7 horns.' So complete military power, horns being the symbol of military might, 7 is the symbol of completion.

[11] *Nero will come back... gone the way the rest are going'*, literally, 'beast that was and is not... and goes to destruction.' This appears to be another reference to the rumour that the murdered Emperor Nero would return. He is seen as a paradigm of all evil emperors, see 13:18.

18

In empires, evil turns:

• responsibility into power for its own sake
• resources into money for its own sake

• relationships into sex for its own sake

Evil is bound to collapse under its own weight, along with its tool of empire. This is the outcome that is revealed to John in this chapter.

[2] *imperial domination was doomed*, literally, 'fallen is Babylon.' Babylon is the symbolic paradigm of empire. Its fall is good news, because it is the end of arrogance and oppression. Its fall tells us that wanton luxury and vice don't have the last word. John is taking up the words of the prophet Isaiah 21:9, 'fallen, fallen is Babylon; all the images of her gods shattered on the ground'. It is the overthrow of idolatry, worshipping things in place of God.

[4] *keep clear...* John picks up Isaiah 48:20, literally, 'come out... from Babylon! Declare to the remotest parts of the earth, God has redeemed his servant.' He's also picking up Jeremiah 51:32, 'come out from her midst. My people, each save yourselves...'

[9] This begins the long lament of the kings and merchants. It uses the great laments of Isaiah 23 and Ezekiel 26-27.

[13] *No market for... bodies, human beings.* The New Testament is implacably against slavery, which was then thought to be essential for society to work. As we have already seen, John's God is the God of liberation: 'with your own blood you purchased a people for God' (5:9). He leads his people through the sea to sing the song of liberation, as in 15:3.

The Fourth Revelation

The victory is won!

Judgement is given in favour of the Messiah's people. We can begin the great song of victory over evil in every form. This is a celebration of Jesus' victory over evil on the cross. Evil used its ultimate weapon, death, and Jesus defeated it. The triumphant celebration is a subversion of triumph. It is an invitation to join him on that road of self-sacrifice.

[20] *judgement.* Babylon (now Rome) is the false accuser of the Messiah's people before God's court. The scene is set in Daniel 7. The court decides against Rome, and Rome's empire, as 'the beast', which will be 'put to death'. John is picking up Deuteronomy 19:16 and following verses, which is also fulfilled by the court's decision. 'If a malicious witness accuses of wrongdoing, do to him as he intended'. The Roman Empire is going to suffer what it intended to do to the Messiah's people.

19

[1] This is the same crowd as in chapters 5 and 7.

Praise to our God, literally, 'Hallelujah' in Hebrew. This is the only chapter in the New Testament where the word occurs. Here John sees Psalm 106:48 realised: 'let all the people... say, amen, praise God!'

[15] *his words cut to the core*, literally, 'from his mouth a sharp sword,' quoting Isaiah 49:2. Also picking up Isaiah 11:4: 'he will strike the earth with the rod of his mouth'.

The Almighty has taken on himself the suffering, literally, 'the wine press of the fury of the wrath of God Almighty.' The wine press comes from Isaiah 62:2 'why are your robes red... I have trodden the wine press alone.' This passage in Isaiah has been transformed by John's experience of Jesus. His blood is now symbolically seen as wine.

[17] *all the nations*, literally, 'all the birds', from Ezekiel 39:17, 'the birds gather all to the sacrificial feast'. This is an image also used for the

nations by Jesus. In his parable of the mustard seed, the birds come to make their home in the tree. The great feast is 'the great feast of God's rule'. Jesus' repeated feasting (with sinners) was a symbolic demondemonstration of this.

[20] *The empire and its idolatry will come to a sticky end,* literally 'the beast and the false prophet were thrown into the lake of fire and sulphur'. While this is particular to Rome, it is symbolic as the fate one day of all imperial domination.

20

[2] *limited its power to harm for as long as needed,* literally, 'bound him for a thousand years.' This calls up Jesus' parable of the binding of the strong man (Matthew 12:29). Jesus accredits his power to drive out demons to his initial defeat of evil in the desert.

[4] *Judgement is already taking place,* literally 'thrones, and those on them given authority to judge'. John is calling up Daniel 7:9 and following verses: 'thrones were set in place and... the court sat in judgement.' For John, Daniel's prophecy of judgement was fulfilled in Jesus' victory on the cross and resurrection. Messiah's people follow him, and those who judge them are now—in the real scheme of things—judging themselves. Daniel 7 is a key chapter in the Hebrew Bible for understanding the whole New Testament.

[6] *those... who now share... the fruit of his resurrection,* literally, 'the first resurrection'. Because John is tracking the book of the prophet Ezekiel, he writes of two resurrections. The first is the resurrection from slavery to evil, given to us now in this life. The second is the final resurrection. It will come in God's time and way with the renewal of the heavens and the earth.

⁸ *led astray and wedded to it*, literally, 'Gog and Magog.' They are called up from Ezekiel 38:2. The people of Magog and Gog their king were feared as a terrible evil threat from the north. John uses them to symbolise evil at its worst.

21

³ *God is at home...* The vision of Genesis 2:1, 'God rested (on the earth) on the seventh day', is now fully realised. God's plan from the beginning was to live with his people on earth. This plan has now been finally accomplished.

⁷ *martyred for bearing witness to me*, literally, 'conquer.' They will conquer evil in the way Jesus conquered evil, on the cross.

⁸ *future is bleak*, literally, 'thrown in the lake of fire and sulphur'. It is impossible to find words for what those who worship evil bring on themselves. Their whole scenario is too appalling and tragic to contemplate. John's symbolic language attempts to describe its real significance.

destroy their own future, literally, 'the second death.' Choosing the destroyer and the way of destruction will lead finally to self-destruction.

¹² *impregnable to fear*, literally, 'a great high wall'. It is a symbolic city so protected that no enemy could capture it. This is reinforced by verse 17 similarly.

¹⁶ *include the whole world*, literally, '1,500 miles,' (the contemporary equivalent to John's measurement). It is symbolically the extent of John's world—roughly the whole of the Roman Empire.

²² *There is no temple* because the whole earth and heavens are now God's temple—the place where God dwells.

¹ *love of God in Jesus flowing*, literally, 'river... from the throne of God and the Lamb.' The river combines Ezekiel 47:1 'water flowing down from under... the altar'; Zechariah 14:8 'living waters will flow out of Jerusalem'; Psalm 46:4 'river whose streams make glad the city of God'; and Psalm 36:8 'from your house you give them drink from the river'. The river is the self-sacrificial love of the Lamb, Jesus, picked up again from chapter 14:20.

² *fed the life*, literally, 'on either side of the river is the tree of life.' John's story is of course the conclusion of God's plan from the beginning. The garden-city-paradise (of which the Jerusalem temple had been a sign) has the tree of life from the garden of Eden, Genesis 3:22, flourishing for ever.

heal the wounds of the nations. The vision of the New Jerusalem, the new society, carries a double meaning. It is a vision of the future for humanity. But it has already started with the Messiah's followers. Yet it has still to come (fully), though it is now already here!

⁶ *It is already in process*, literally, 'what must soon take place'. John's whole book carries the utmost urgency. The choice and actions that need to be taken are vital right now. The final outcome is of course still in God's hands, and may be a long way off, John's 1,000 years of chapter 20. It is an indeterminate period, but one that will certainly end one day.

⁸ *began to worship the messenger*, literally, 'I fell to worship before the feet of the messenger'. The whole issue of John's book is whether people would worship God or idols. But there is no simple division between 'us' and 'them'. All may be tempted to worship idols, and to go down that road. John is conscious that he equally can fall for making

idols of people or things that are less than God. But he sees doing so as fatal, and has the urgency to turn from it.

[10] *Don't keep these prophecies secret*, literally, 'Do not seal up the words of this prophecy'. This is in direct contrast to Daniel 12:4 'Keep the words secret and the book sealed'. Daniel is told that the words apply to the 'end times', but now the 'end times' have already arrived, with Jesus.

If you enjoyed Revelation Unpacked...

Also by the same translator:
Jesus Decoded: a first historical translation of Luke's Gospel

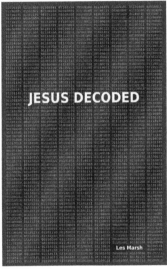

'Truth is stranger than fiction,' they say. If so, the true story of Jesus of Nazareth must be the strangest story of all. When first told, it set the world on fire. Those caught with it were fed to lions. Rulers said it 'turned the world upside down.'

Read *Jesus Decoded* as you would the story of any other human. You may be amazed at what you find out.

'I think each generation has to have a go at this kind of thing... to bring out the original flavour in ways which make sense today' - Bishop Tom Wright

Lightning Source UK Ltd.
Milton Keynes UK
UKOW06f1544091015

260201UK00001B/3/P